I hope that you enjoy the activities in this book.

Thank you to those who helped me put this together.

Thanks Karlene, Selina, and Stephanie.

ACTIVITY BOOK

SOFIE at BAT

Written by Suzan Johnson
Illustrated by Susan Shorter

ISBN-13: 978-1947082946
ISBN-10: 1947082949

Ordering Information:
To order additional copies of this book, please visit Amazon or shjstories.com
Also available on Createspace at: https://www.createspace.com/9066353.

Sofie at Bat Activity Book.
© Suzan Johnson.
First Printing, 2018.

Acrostic Poem

Directions: Create an Acrostic Poem using the letters of the title, "Sofie at Bat."

S

O

F

I

E

A

T

B

A

T

Fill in the Missing Words

Directions: Use the book, "Sofie at Bat" or your imagination to fill the blanks in the paragraph from the story.

Sofie hit every ball her _____

pitched. Some of them went _____

the _____. Sofie was so

_____

that she called her best _____

from the team and told him the marvelous

_____.

2

Color in the PATTERNS

3

Tic Tac Toe

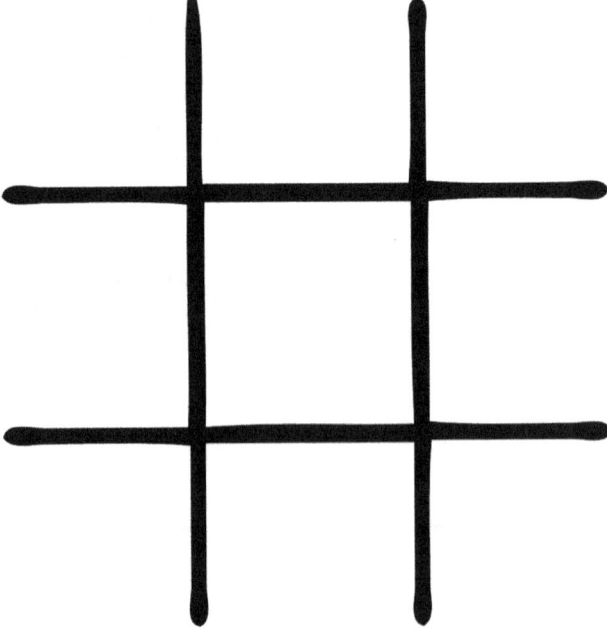

Color in the PATTERNS

Finish the Maze

6

Tic Tac Toe

8

Sketch and Color YOUR own Character

Compare TWO Sports

Directions: Compare any TWO sports that you know of..

NAME _____   NAME _____

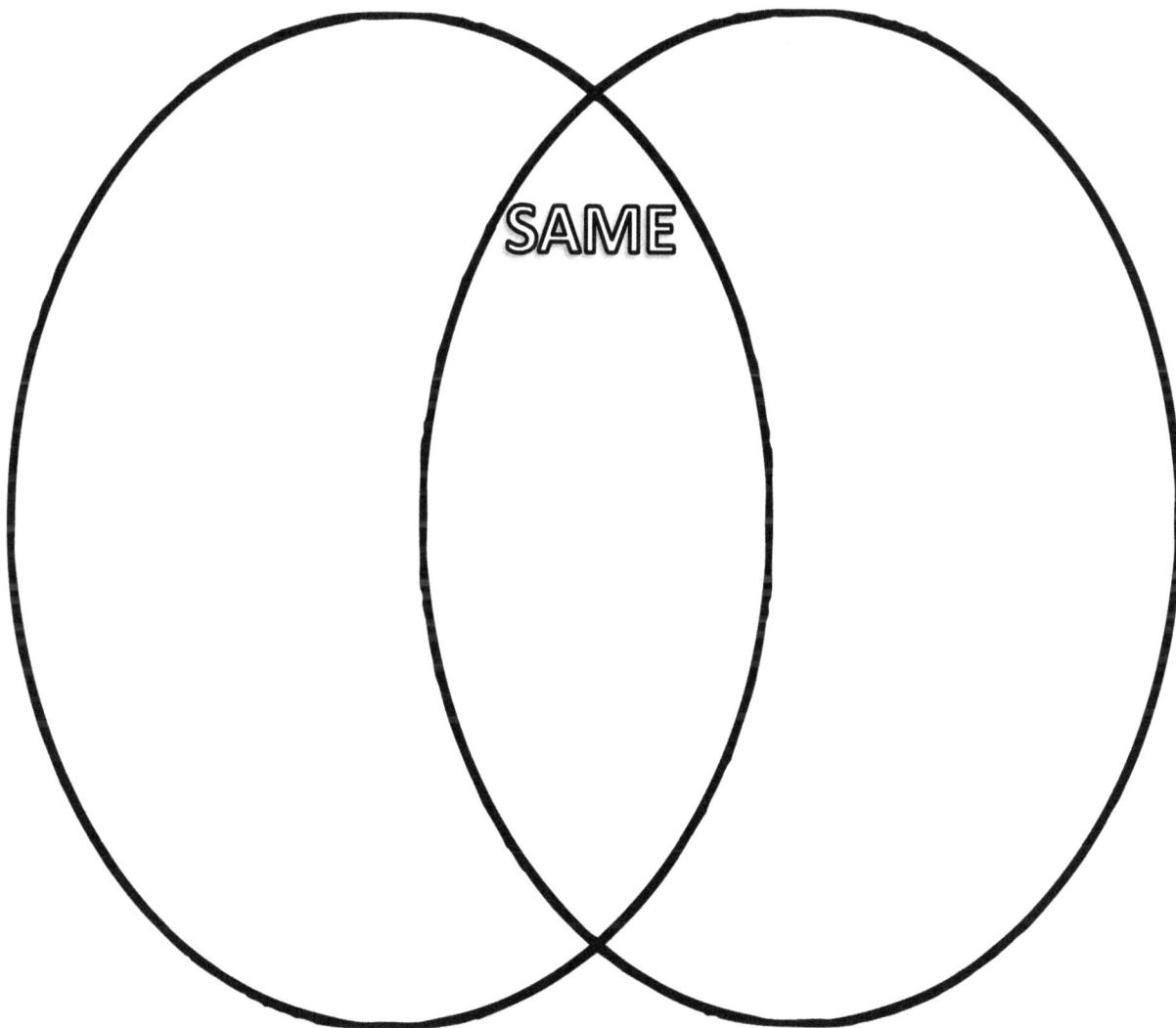

SAME

13

Compare TWO Characters

Directions: Compare any TWO characters from the story, "Sofie at Bat."

NAME _____   NAME _____

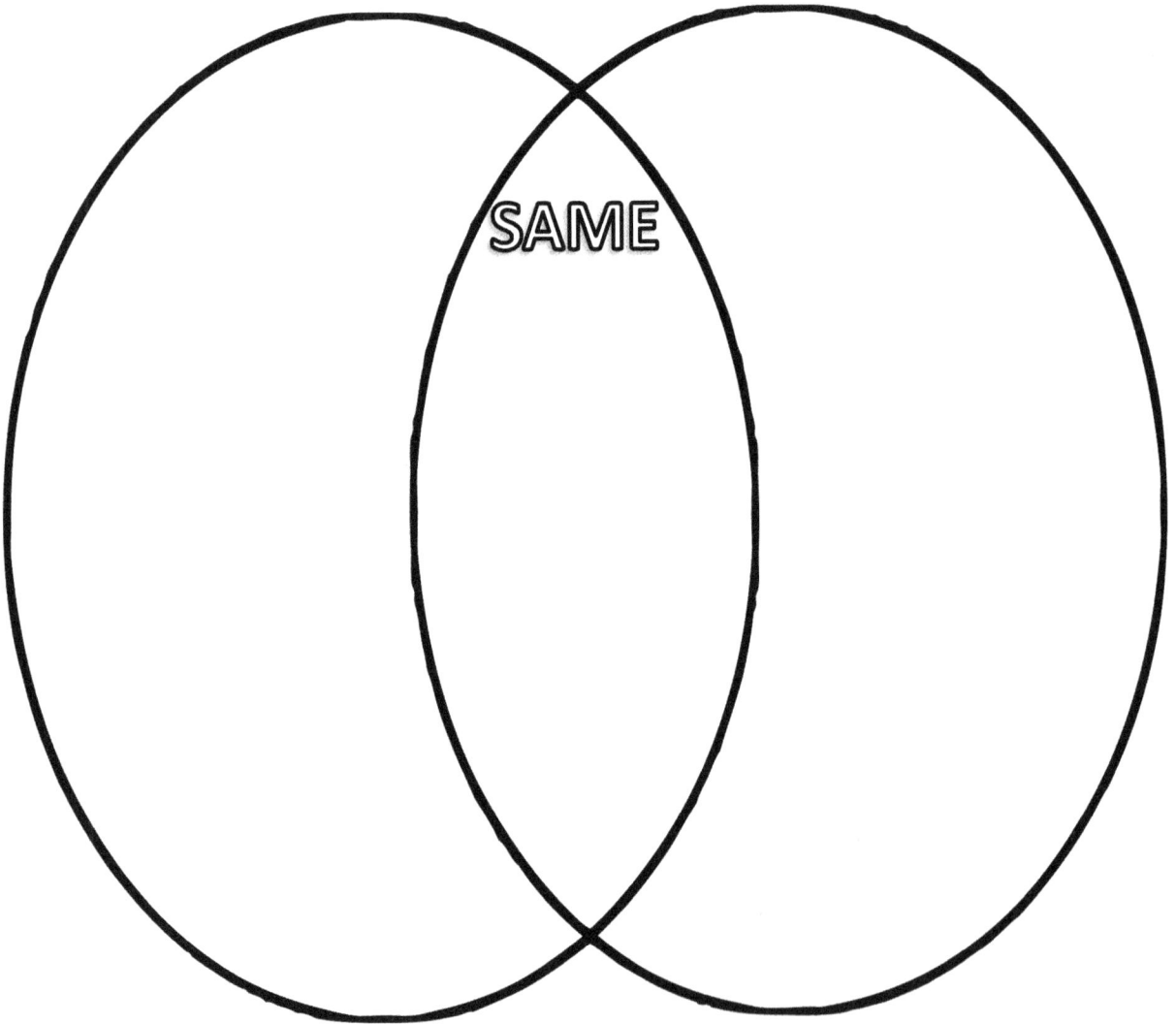

SAME

14

Tic Tac Toe

Sketch and Color a Character

Sketch and Color YOUR own Character

Create a MAP of the PLACES in the story
(Label your MAP)

Connect the Dots

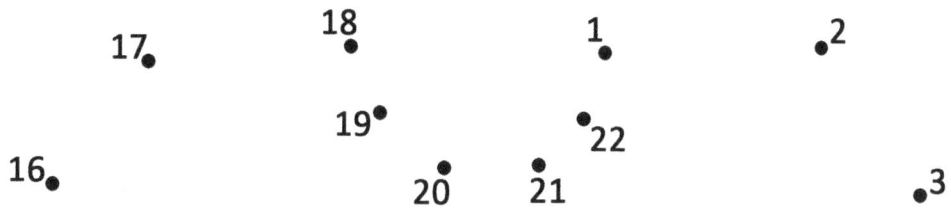

17• 18• 1• •2

19• •22

16• 20 21 •3

EAGLES

1

•15 13• 6• 4•

14• •5

•7

12•

11•

•8

10• •9

Draw Your Favorite Part of the Story

Make-Up Your Own Story: Change the Sport

Directions: Retell the story after you change the sport from "softball" to _____.

_____

_____

_____

_____

_____

_____

_____

_____

_____

_____

21

_____

_____

_____

_____

_____

_____

_____

_____

_____

_____

_____

_____

Make-Up Your Own Story: Change the Sport

Directions: Retell the story after you change the sport from "softball" to _____.

_____

_____

_____

_____

_____

_____

_____

_____

_____

_____

_____

23

WORD SCRAMBLE

Directions: Unscramble the words that can be found the story " Sofie at Bat".

RSSAKH   _____

EELSGA   _____

FABOTLLS   _____

OSEFI   _____

EET   _____

ALLB   _____

ABT   _____

WORD SEARCH

```
Y L O N T Y T X F T E A M J H H M Z D
J M O F Z K O T A R C V V M Q K S J W
E S I B E K M D D U O E B A R Y O P S
A D H M B K M T S S Q S H A R K S N W
G G B A T J Y G I U M C A N G A S S A
L K S R E S W L R S A U R S C X M G F
E S E N O J V S Z O E A V E I J K N A
S O F I E I E N C W P N U E U V D I C
J T S P I X A F R O Y K O H B G M N P
T N P Z I M B J M B A L L J U B X N A
L Z R C D B H W Y H T J J P I J F I P
I U M P I R E Z O I K W N W P Y H R I
```

WORDS

BALL	SHARKS	BAT	SOFIE
COACH	TEAM	EAGLES	TOMMY
INNINGS	UMPIRE	JONES	PAPI

26

Design Your Own Jersey

Directions: Create your own team jersey.

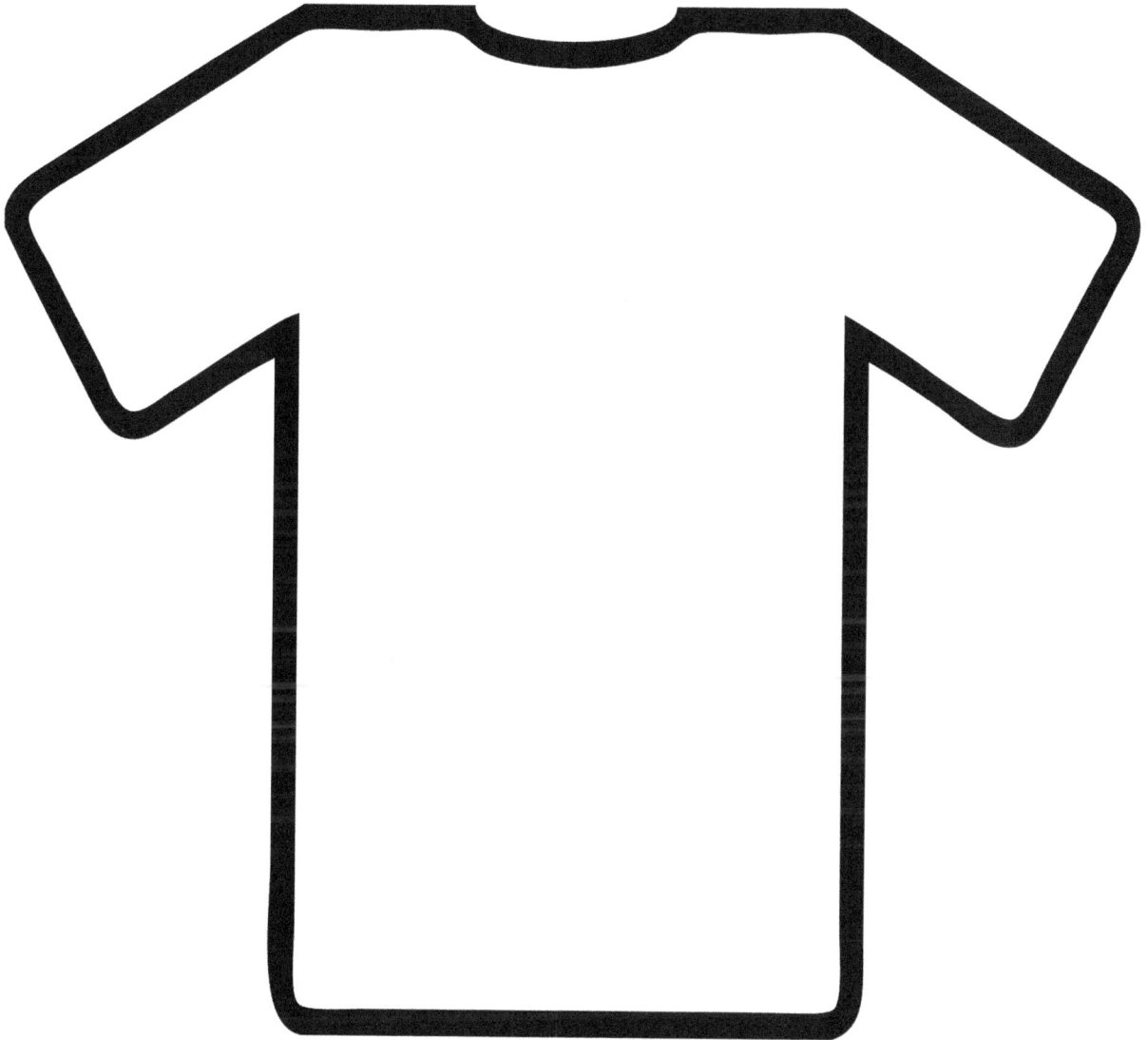

Story Map

Directions: Complete the story map with information from the book.

Characters (who?):	Setting (when and where?):	Problem (what is wrong?):
Events to Solve the Problem:	**Solution:**	**Picture of your FAVORITE part:**

Sequence

Directions: After reading the story, fill in the chart with the sequence from the book. Write and/or Draw what happened at the beginning, middle, and end. Then tell the moral of the story, in other words, what did you learn.

Beginning:

Middle:

End:

Moral of the story:

Answers

Word Scramble:

SHARKS

EAGLES

SOFTBALL

SOFIE

TEE

BALL

BAT

Maze Answer:

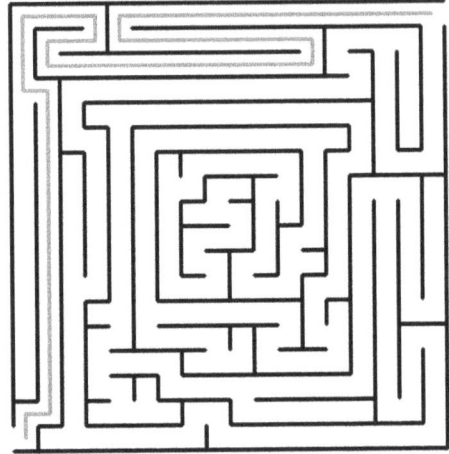

Crossword Answer:

```
Y L O N T Y T X F T E A M J H H M Z D
J M O F Z K O T A R C V V M Q K S J W
E S I B E K M D D U O E B A R Y O P S
A D H M B K M T S S Q S H A R K S N W
G G B A T J Y G I U M C A N G A S S A
L K S R E S W L R S A U R S C X M G F
E S E N O J V S Z O E A V E I J K N A
S O F I E I E N C W P N U E U V D I C
J T S P I X A F R O Y K O H B G M N P
T N P Z I M B J M B A L L J U B X N A
L Z R C D B H W Y H T J J P I J F I P
I U M P I R E Z O I K W N W P Y H R I
```

Connect the Dots Answer:

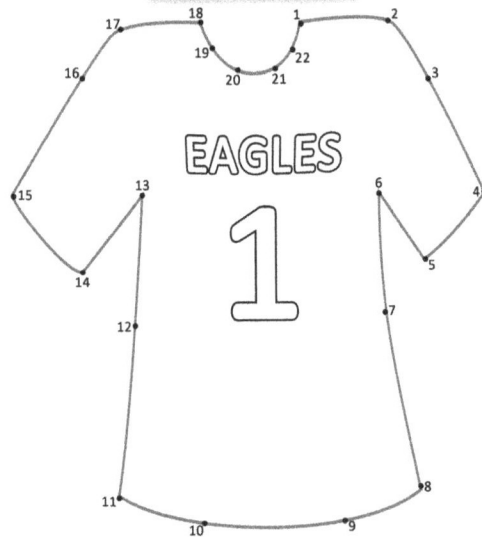

More from the Author

Get your copies from Amazon.com or shjstories.com.

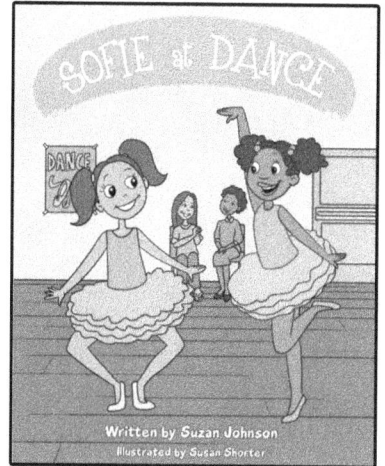
SOFIE at DANCE
Written by Suzan Johnson
Illustrated by Susan Shorter

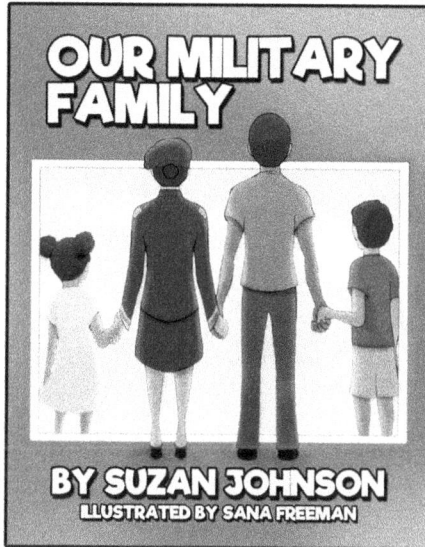
OUR MILITARY FAMILY
BY SUZAN JOHNSON
ILLUSTRATED BY SANA FREEMAN

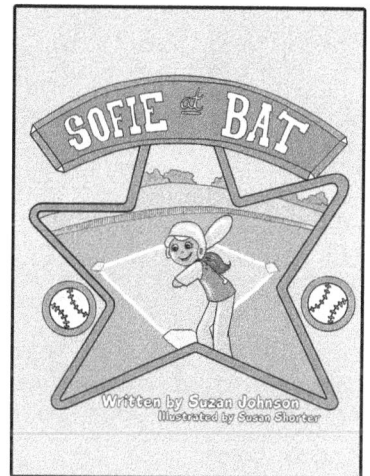
My Heartbeats
Written By Suzan Johnson
Illustrated by Selina Ahmed at True Beginnings Publishing

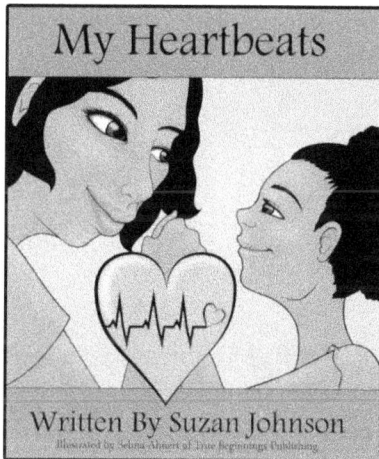
SOFIE at BAT
Written by Suzan Johnson
Illustrated by Susan Shorter

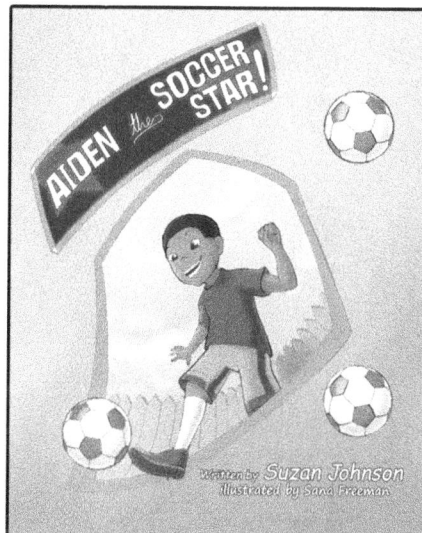
AIDEN the SOCCER STAR!
Written by Suzan Johnson
Illustrated by Sana Freeman

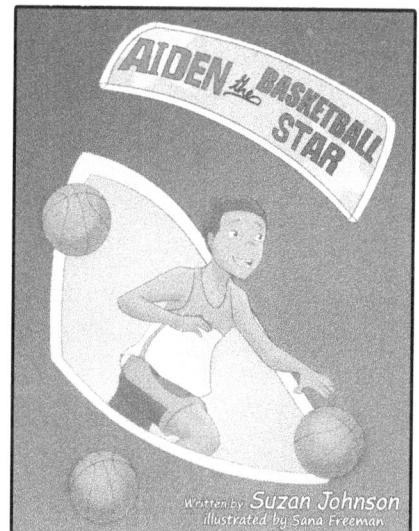
AIDEN the BASKETBALL STAR
Written by Suzan Johnson
Illustrated by Sana Freeman

www.ingramcontent.com/pod-product-compliance
Lightning Source LLC
Chambersburg PA
CBHW081307040426

42452CB00014B/2692